Fairburn's Edition of The Trial Between Sir Jacob Astley, Bart. Plaintiff, and Thomas Garth, Defendant, for Criminal Conversation With The Plaintiff's Wife; Including The Whole of The Recriminatory Evidence of Mrs. Richardson and Her Girls, &c &c.

Anonymous

Fairburn's Edition of The Trial Between Sir Jacob Astley, Bart. Plaintiff, and Thomas Garth, Defendant, for Criminal Conversation With The Plaintiff's Wife; Including The Whole of The Recriminatory Evidence of Mrs. Richardson and Her Girls, &c &c.

The Making of Modern Law collection of legal archives constitutes a genuine revolution in historical legal research because it opens up a wealth of rare and previously inaccessible sources in legal, constitutional, administrative, political, cultural, intellectual, and social history. This unique collection consists of three extensive archives that provide insight into more than 300 years of American and British history. These collections include:

Legal Treatises, 1800-1926: over 20,000 legal treatises provide a comprehensive collection in legal history, business and economics, politics and government.

Trials, 1600-1926: nearly 10,000 titles reveal the drama of famous, infamous, and obscure courtroom cases in America and the British Empire across three centuries.

Primary Sources, 1620-1926: includes reports, statutes and regulations in American history, including early state codes, municipal ordinances, constitutional conventions and compilations, and law dictionaries.

These archives provide a unique research tool for tracking the development of our modern legal system and how it has affected our culture, government, business – nearly every aspect of our everyday life. For the first time, these high-quality digital scans of original works are available via print-on-demand, making them readily accessible to libraries, students, independent scholars, and readers of all ages.

The BiblioLife Network

This project was made possible in part by the BiblioLife Network (BLN), a project aimed at addressing some of the huge challenges facing book preservationists around the world. The BLN includes libraries, library networks, archives, subject matter experts, online communities and library service providers. We believe every book ever published should be available as a high-quality print reproduction; printed on-demand anywhere in the world. This insures the ongoing accessibility of the content and helps generate sustainable revenue for the libraries and organizations that work to preserve these important materials.

The following book is in the "public domain" and represents an authentic reproduction of the text as printed by the original publisher. While we have attempted to accurately maintain the integrity of the original work, there are sometimes problems with the original work or the micro-film from which the books were digitized. This can result in minor errors in reproduction. Possible imperfections include missing and blurred pages, poor pictures, markings and other reproduction issues beyond our control. Because this work is culturally important, we have made it available as part of our commitment to protecting, preserving, and promoting the world's literature.

GUIDE TO FOLD-OUTS MAPS and OVERSIZED IMAGES

The book you are reading was digitized from microfilm captured over the past thirty to forty years. Years after the creation of the original microfilm, the book was converted to digital files and made available in an online database.

In an online database, page images do not need to conform to the size restrictions found in a printed book. When converting these images back into a printed bound book, the page sizes are standardized in ways that maintain the detail of the original. For large images, such as fold-out maps, the original page image is split into two or more pages

Guidelines used to determine how to split the page image follows:

• Some images are split vertically; large images require vertical and horizontal splits.
• For horizontal splits, the content is split left to right.
• For vertical splits, the content is split from top to bottom.
• For both vertical and horizontal splits, the image is processed from top left to bottom right.

CJR. QUIETEM

Sr John Hall of
Dunglass Baronet

FAIRBURN'S EDITION

OF THE

TRIAL

BETWEEN

SIR JACOB ASTLEY, BART.

AND

THOMAS GARTH,

FOR

Crim. Con.

ILLUSTRATED WITH

A CARICATURE ENGRAVING

Price One Shilling. 1s. 6d.

JUL 1 3 1932

FAIRBURN, Printer,
Broadway, Ludgate Hill

Crim. Con. Extraordinary!

FAIRBURN'S EDITION

OF THE

TRIAL

BETWEEN

Sir JACOB ASTLEY, Bart.

PLAINTIFF,

AND

THOMAS GARTH,

DEFENDANT,

FOR

Criminal Conversation

WITH THE PLAINTIFF'S WIFE

Including the Whole of the

RECRIMINATORY EVIDENCE

OF

MRS RICHARDSON AND HER GIRLS, &c &c

THE

SPEECHES OF COUNSEL,

AND THE

JUDGE'S CHARGE TO THE JURY

AT FULL LENGTH

*Tried before Lord Chief Justice Best, and a Special Jury,
in the Court of Common Pleas, Westminster, Feb. 19, 1827*

———◆———

ILLUSTRATED WITH A LARGE COLOURED CARICATURE

———◆———

LONDON
Published by JOHN FAIRBURN, Broadway, Ludgate-Hill

TRIAL, &c.

Sir JACOB ASTLEY, Bart.
VERSUS
THOMAS GARTH

THIS was an action brought by the plaintiff to recover compensation in damages for the injury he had sustained at the defendant's hands, for criminal conversation with his wife. The damages were laid at 12 000l.

COUNSEL FOR THE PLAINTIFF.

Mr SCARLETT	Mr Common Serjeant DENMAN,
Mr Serjeant TADDY,	Mr G BEST

COUNSEL FOR THE DEFENDANT

Mr Serjeant VAUGHAN,	Mr BROUGHAM,
Mr Serjeant WILDE,	Mr CHITTY

Mr BEST opened the pleadings. The declaration stated that the plaintiff in this cause was Sir Jacob Astley, the defendant was Mr Thomas Garth, who had seduced and held criminal conversation with, the plaintiff's wife. To this he pleaded "Not guilty."

Mr SCARLETT stated the case. He said that he had the honour of appearing for the plaintiff in this cause, who had been reduced to the painful necessity of appealing to a Court of Justice in one of those cases which, if a man had a choice of the events of his own life, would be the very last in which he would be engaged. The plaintiff here sought to recover such compensation as the jury should think it right and necessary to give to a man who had lost the tenderest companion with which the life of man could be blest, who had lost the dearest wife and most affectionate companion, all by the seduction and artifice of him who was the defendant in the cause this day. Cases of this nature had in our

P

time, become frequently the subject of discussion in our
Courts of Justice, and the learned gentleman did not know
whether an advocate who attempted to describe them in
their strongest colours might not be accused of encroaching
on the rules of good taste He should make no such attempt
but would state simply the facts of the case which without
exaggeration and on its true grounds would call on them
to make ample compensation for the injury which the plaintiff had sustained He apprehended that the jury were
aware that in such cases it was a general rule with advocates,
in order that they might ascertain in some measure the loss
that a plaintiff had sustained, to describe what had been the
demerits of the defendant but, whatever their demerits
might be, there was no just cause for such statements He
should not in the present instance attack the character of
the defendant except so far as the truth of the case required .
but this he had mentioned only as a caution to the jury
Sir Jacob Astley was descended from a good and ancient
family, and was possessed of a splendid fortune During the
period in which he was pursuing the course of his education
at Oxford, he became first acquainted with Lady Astley, who
was the daughter of Sir Henry Dashwood He was, at that
time, of an age when love for an individual takes the deep-
est root in the heart and such were the accomplishments of
this lady that his affection was formed for her it continued
to increase during his residence at Sir Henry's house, and being returned by her, their mutual affection was ultimately
rewarded by their marriage, which took place in March,
1819 he having been a few months of age when he became
the husband of this lady which appeared to be the happiest
event in their lives The lady was about six or eight months
older than Sir Jacob her beauty was great, and her manners
elegant and captivating They were married in the presence
of their dearest friends, and the friendship which had always
existed between the two families appeared, in consequence
of this event, to be more firmly cemented , and up to the unhappy time in which the defendant would be brought before
the notice of the jury, they had lived in a state of uninterrupted felicity Immediately after his marriage, Sir Jacob
took his bride first to Cumberland were they resided some
time after that into Scotland , from whence, after some
stay, they proceeded to Sir Jacob's house, at Melton Constable, in Norfolk, were they resided a short time, and then
came to town to his house, were Lady Astley was surrounded
with every comfort that fortune could supply The alliances
on both sides were attached to her, and particularly the
family of her husband Her conduct was every thing that
could delight a husband, and he should call witnesses who

would fully bear out this statement that Sir Jacob's affection and attention towards her had continued up to the time when the unfortunate event took place. The learned Advocate wished he could state that the affection which Sir Jacob had formed for her, and which had taken so deep a root in his heart, had ceased to exist but he feared it would make a lasting impression on his mind and cast a shade over the latter days of his life. Her accomplishments had been admired, and justly so, they had attracted the attention of Sir Jacob at a time when they were calculated to make the strongest impression and when it was impossible to resist them early attachments were known to be the strongest and most lasting, while those that follow at a later period are cooler, and may be shaken off almost at will, never taken so strong a hold as the first. It happened that in May, 1826 Sir Jacob who had then lately purchased a new mansion in Grosvenor-street, and being desirous of placing the embellishments of the dwelling house under the immediate controul of Lady Astley, gratified her by coming to town. It was at this time she first saw the defendant, Mr Garth. It happened, that Sir Jacob having been in Leicestershire, for the purpose of hunting, accompanied by his lady, he formed an acquaintance with Mr Garth, in consequence of hunting with the same hounds — this, however, was a mere acquaintance, as they never visited each other nor had Lady Astley ever seen him. As has been stated she came to town and took possession of her house in Grosvenor-street where she continued to reside until June last, without separation from her husband. Mr Garth was a lieutenant in the Guards, and was in the habit of seeing and being in much fashionable life kept a handsome equipage and was possessed of a good fortune. A short time after their arrival in town, this gentleman called on Sir Jacob on the ground of their former acquaintance, and became one of the regular visitors at the house. While visiting at the house he paid every attention to Lady Astley, but not such as in any way excited the suspicion of the family. The Jury would all remember that at this period there was a great stir in the country caused by the General Election. During this time Sir Jacob (who was not so well acquainted with the place as he, Mr Scarlett was) was persuaded to offer himself as a candidate for Seaford, and in June he left town for that place, accompanied by another gentleman and a clergyman with whom he was very intimate, who resided in his family as chaplain. They arrived at Seaford and remained a few days returning however in the first week in June. Up to this time nothing had occurred that could excite the attention of the family. Mr

Garth had certainly accompanied Lady Astley to the Park, and had been with her to the assemblies at which she had gone; but so had many others. The beauty and affability of Lady Astley could not fail of being extremely attractive to gentlemen. A short time after Sir Jacob's return from Seaford he was compelled to leave town, in order to attend at the Bedford election, for which place his friend Mr M,Queen was a candidate, and from thence he went to the Norwich election in which he was interested. These movements necessarily took some time, and it would be proved that during that time Mr Garth's attentions became more particular, but still not so particularly so as to cause any remark from any part of the family. They had gone to the Opera and other places of public amusement together, but there certainly had never been any conduct observed between them that could be termed at all indecorous or that in any way excited the attention of his friends, no remark whatever having been made. When Sir Jacob arrived in town, it became necessary to make some arrangements for leaving town, and one of the children being rather indisposed Lady Astley was desirous of going to the coast of Sussex, in preference to returning to Norfolk. Worthing was accordingly fixed on, and a house being taken, the children were sent there to remain until she could join them. At this time Sir Jacob had an engagement at Yarmouth, where the races were being celebrated and he asked Lady Astley if she would like to accompany him there, but she preferred remaining in town, as she should be nearer to her children, whom she intended shortly to join. It was, indeed, very natural that she should prefer joining her children at Worthing, to making a journey to Yarmouth, for the sake of seeing horse-racing, a pleasure in which she could take no delight. Sir Jacob, whose greatest pleasure was to gratify his wife, could not deny her her request, and did not insist on her accompanying him. Indeed it could not have entered into the head of a husband that a wife, with whom he had lived so long and so happily, had at that time any intention of separating from him. Sir Jacob, understanding from her that she intended to join her children at Worthing, said he would join her at that place on his return.— While Sir Jacob was gone to Yarmouth, Mr Elwyn, the clergyman who had accompanied him to Seaford, and who had just taken the children to Worthing, returned to town, where he met the mother of Lady Astley, and then her brother the Rev Augustus Dashwood. It was late in the evening, however, when he arrived, and the Rev Mr Dashwood did not sleep in the house. Lady Astley and a sister of Sir Jacob's were not at home when he arrived. It appeared that they had been out in the carriage, accompanied by Mr Garth, they returned home at rather a late hour and after a short time again left in the carriage accompanied by Mr Garth, and went to Vauxhall This certainly appeared rather odd to Mr Elwyn, but he made no remark thinking that as they had been riding together in the Park they might also go to Vauxhall Shortly after this he received a letter from the Dowager Lady Astley which excited a remark from him which the succeeding events brought to his recollection. The Dowager Lady Astley not knowing whether Mr Elwyn was in town had addressed two letters to him to the same effect, directing one to town and the other to Melton Constable Mr Elwyn received the letter in town the contents of it surprised him exceedingly, as the Dowager Lady Astley informed him that the general conduct of Mr Garth and being so frequently with Lady Astley, had excited some remarks in town Being unwilling to hurt the feelings of her son, she thought best first to inform his confidential friend in order to make some inquiries, and to prevent the busy hand of slander, which in this large town is too readily raised to the injury of a beautiful and accomplished woman Mr Elwyn, comparing the contents of this extraordinary letter with what he had himself seen, and calling to mind the visit to Vauxhall, thought it would be best to acquaint Sir Jacob in a delicate way with what he had heard and seen For this purpose, he left town, without having seen or in any way acquainting Lady Astley with what he had heard but left her brother, the Rev Mr Dashwood, to explain every thing to her When he arrived in Norfolk, he found that Sir Jacob had about that time received the duplicate to the letter which he had received in town and knowing it to be his mother's hand-writing, he had taken the liberty of opening it and its contents were the first information he had ever received from any human being that could cast any imputation on the unsullied character of his wife Having read this letter before Mr Elwyn arrived their first conversation was as to what should be done to protect his wife, and to prevent any slander from being thrown upon her It was thought by Mr Elwyn and Sir Jacob, that the safest way to proceed would be not to let it be supposed that Sir Jacob had any suspicion of her integrity, and that it would be best for him not to go to town, as it would only tend to confirm the reports that had been spread It was agreed that Mr Elwyn should go alone to town, and request her to return to Melton Constable — He accordingly came to town, and saw Mr Dashwood, with whom he had some conversation, which the learned gentleman could not relate to the jury, as he had no evidence to

bear it out. Lady Astley had not the slightest symptom of
a guilty conscience Mr Elwyn had some conversation with
her, and it was agreed that the horses and carriage should
be ready on the next morning to convey them into the country, and she appeared to second the views of her husband
in the preservation of her honour Mr Dashwood did not
sleep in the house, and in the evening retired to his lodg-
ings Mr Elwyn went to bed, as also did Miss Astley,
who during Sir Jacob s absence was in the habit of sleep-
ing in Lady Astley's apartment When she got into her
room she was much surprised to find no one there, as she
supposed Lady Astley had retired to bed some time previous
She immediately rang the bell, and called the servants, for
the purpose of making a search after her, but she was no-
where to be found Mr Elwyn was called up, and Mr
Dashwood sent to Their suspicions immediately fell on
Mr Garth and they caused enquiry to be made at his lodg-
ings The reply was that he was not at home that evening
They then enquired of a watchman, who was seated in a
box and who was known to the family, his wife being a
washerwoman, and had several times shown little attentions to Lady Astley by sending her nosegays and trifles of
that description, whether she had seen any body about the
house that evening He said he had seen Garth's carriage
draw up with the horses' heads towards Davies Street, and
about half-past 12 o'clock he saw somebody come out of Sir
Jacob s house and get into the carriage which immediately
drove off at a rapid rate The conclusion was, naturally,
that she had eloped with Mr Garth and on the next day
but one, she was seen with him by Mr Elwyn, and had
since been seen in the neighbourhood of Salt-hill from
time to time, so that there could be no doubt of an adulter-
ous intercourse The fact of their living together was no-
torious, therefore there could be no doubt on that head.
The question now to be considered was in the hands of the
jury it was for them to say how the honour of Sir Jacob
had been injured and it was for them to decide what compensation should be given to him for the loss of that uninterrupted happiness and felicity he had enjoyed up to the
period in which the unhappy event took place which
was the subject of discussion this day The learned
Advocate had no doubt that the jury were not strangers
to the reports which had been circulated with regard
to Sir Jacob Astley, but he defied his learned friends
to prove by evidence that a more affectionate husband ever
found his way into a Court of Justice nor ever met the seducer of his wife face to face with more diffidence but the
scandal which was so much circulated in this country, and

which in this instance had been aided by the press, had compelled him to come into Court, in order to vindicate his character from the aspersions which had been thrown out against it and it was more for this purpose than the recovery of heavy damages that he presented himself before them this day. He would now proceed to relate by what means Mr Garth had been successful in seducing the unhappy lady. It appeared, that the term of their acquaintance was not long, and this might probably be argued against her this day, and they all knew how true was the excellent old maxim ' that the best part of virtue was discretion." But most women would lend an ear and it was natural to the sex to listen to a man who was well acquainted with the ways of the world, who had been accustomed to its gayest scenes, and who was able to whisper in her ear some tale of scandal relating to her husband—such a man, if there were any, was able in too short a time to break down the fence which had been raised in protection of virtue and was able to reduce a woman from an honourable life to become a mere object for the gratification of his lust, afterwards looking on her with horror and disgust. Mr Garth, when he commenced his intrigue with this unhappy lady found her a woman surrounded with every comfort that her heart could desire two lovely children, and a husband who had never given her any cause of uneasiness, possessed of a splendid fortune, and encircled within a family who doated on her, and whose company must have ever been delightful to her. In this state she was found by Mr Garth happy beyond the usual fate of her sex. What was her situation now that she had given way to the wiles of an artful seducer? All her tenderest ties broken her children, instead of being a delight to her were only to be thought on with eternal shame and torment. He had robbed Sir Jacob of a most tender and affectionate wife, and had degraded her to the state he had described. What reparation could Mr Garth make to-day? Would he trick up any little anecdote or any little foible in the character of the husband on which to ground a defence? Would he first seduce a woman who had lived as a tender wife for a period of six years and with whose husband he had been on terms of intimacy would he then turn against him and make use of every trifling occurrence for the purpose of injuring his honour? It might be said that Lady Astley had too easily fallen a prey to his seductive wiles. The learned advocate admitted it every woman who had fallen in that way had fallen too easily a prey. But they all knew that there were men in the world, who, by their artifice and cunning and polite attention to women, were able to effect in a few

months that which could not be effected by the generality
of men in as many years   But if it could be shown by Mr
Garth that any of the conduct on her side was other than
the most decorous   if he could show that the husband had
alienated himself from her   if he could show that the children were wanting in affection towards her   if he could
show that the lady was willing to leave her husband, would
it in any way defend his conduct ?   But it would be shown
that her conduct previous to this event had always been
strictly virtuous   Even admitting that it had not, what defence could it be to Mr Garth, who had robbed him of a
wife and mother to his children ?   Surely it could not   The
learned gentleman was almost afraid of stating his opinion
on this case, lest it should appear, in this age of gaiety and
fashion, like old morality   Cases of this nature were, in
this age   treated with a kind of levity, and graver opi-
nions appeared to be gradually yielding to this general
feeling   But in a Court of Justice, where men look
on the sober realities of life, by what rule were they to
judge of the conduct of men   who when in company with
married women   should surround them with their many assi-
duities, and take advantage of their affability ?   He considered that a man was bound to approach a married woman
at some distance, and with some reverence   The jury would
not be discharging their duty to the public, if they did not
by their verdict shew that a married woman was to be protected from any approach that was not respectful   No man
should tell him (Mr Scarlett) that Mr Garth was a young
man in the hey-day of life   at the time when the passions
were strongest   It would be proved, that while he was himself carrying on this scene of seduction   he was backed by
others who appeared to be making similar attempts on other
branches of the family   but this did not partake of the present case, and he would go no farther into it   He understood that his learned friend intended to argue that this Mr
Garth was a young man   raw and ignorant, unpractised in
the ways of the world   at a time of life when an impression
made by a beautiful and accomplished woman was likely to
prove irresistible, and should on the strength of that impression advance improperly towards them   when they would be
found to be women and not angels   He understood that his
learned friend meant to contend that a person more advanced
in years could look on a married woman   could associate
with her   and yet have the power of checking any improper
feeling towards her   which would be impossible for a young
man to do   who, at the sight of a young and beautiful woman   was unable to control the passion he felt for her, and
that passion might be such as he should be unable to resist

But what was it that protected the sister from the brutal passion of the brother, or the daughter from that of the father?
What was it, but the deep sense of moral and religious duty
which is planted in us, and which raises a barrier strong and
impassable? Not quite so strong, but of the same kind, was
the barrier between a man and a married woman, and he
who passed that barrier, did not do it from the effects of a
hasty and sudden passion, but he did it by means of cool deliberation, having calculated and well considered the pro-
jects by which he was to succeed in gratifying his passion
What compensation could be given to a husband who had
lost his wife—his honour—by the cool deliberation of another, it would be for the jury to say He believed that Mr
Garth was about 28 years of age but he had the appearance of being much younger, and although really a young
man, he was one well versed in the scenes and occurrences
of fashionable life He was an officer in the Guards, and
like most gentlemen of his profession was partial to, and
was frequently in company with, the ladies But he had
not, like Sir Jacob Astley, formed an early attachment,—he
had never felt the strength of the first impression of real
esteem made on the heart of a man by a beautiful woman.
He had not, like Sir Jacob, married in his younger days
But Mr Garth was a gentleman who well knew the weak
side of the female sex,—every pretty woman was more or
less fond of flattery, nor could she be well otherwise But
the learned counsel would ask, why a man should feel himself entitled to break down the fence of virtue, and unblush-
ingly attack the honour of a wife, and seek to destroy the
peace and happiness of a family? This had been the conduct
of Mr Garth, and he had done an irreparable injury to the
husband, who had fondly looked forward to a long and
happy life in the embraces of a virtuous wife But from
this time he was become a cast-away in the world all his
fond hopes blasted, and was now compelled to alter the
whole course of his life, and make new arrangements with
regard to his future existence He had lost a companion for
life and the only reparation the jury could make was in
money and he thought that when they came to reflect on
the injury which had been given, not only to the feelings
but to the honour of the plaintiff,—when they heard proved
what he had stated to them,—they would feel convinced
that that reparation must be heavy He would not dwell
on the theme of Mr Garth's having violated the bonds of
friendship but he would say that he had during his life gone
about seeking whom he might devour In the present instance he had succeeded in degrading a woman from a state
of happiness and felicity to a state of misery, wretchedness,
and despair He would not longer trespass on the time of

the jury, but would call his witnesses, and leave the case in their hands, not doubting that they would give such damages as they should think proper, in punishment of a crime which was now become too frequent in this country

Mr Hall produced the marriage certificate, and proved that they were married at St George's, Hanover-square

The certificate was then put in and read. It described the marriage of Sir Jacob Astley, Bart of Melton Constable, in the county of Norfolk, to Georgiana Caroline, daughter of Sir Henry Dashwood, of Glocestester-place, by special licence, by the Archbishop of Canterbury, on the 22d of March, 1819 to which there were twelve signatures

The Dowager Lady Astley examined by Mr Serjeant TADDY

I am the mother of Sir Jacob Astley he was married in March, 1819, at St George's, Hanover-square He married Miss Georgiana Caroline Dashwood, daughter of Sir Henry Dashwood Sir Jacob had only quitted College (Oxford) the preceding October The acquaintance had been of some time standing The marriage was solemnised with the entire approbation of the two families There was another marriage took place between Sir Jacob's sister (my daughter) and the Rev Mr Dashwood, the brother of my daughter-in-law I have been in the habit of visiting my son's seat in Norfolk, Melton Constable I have had frequent opportunities of witnessing the manner of Sir Jacob and his lady both in the country and in town, and have always found that they lived in the greatest harmony with each other She superintended the family arrangements, and was apparently very happy The conduct of Lady Astley in respect of her family, was every thing we could wish Sir Jacob Astley had two boys—the youngest boy was a year old in March 1825 It was their habit to reside, in the London season, in town Immediately after their marriage, they went into Scotland Till within last year, I had no reason to suppose that on either part there was any abatement of affection I had no reason to suppose it until within three days of their separation Last Christmas twelvemonth, I was staying with my son and daughter, and only left Melton Constable on the 20th January 1826 I was three months in the house previous to that period I have had opportunities of witnessing their conduct towards each other, and perceiving every marked attention on both sides She was extremely kind to her children, and took that interest and attention in them that an affectionate mother would do When I left Melton Constable, I came immediately to town The whole family resided there When I came to London, Sir Jacob and his lady went into Leicestershire They came to town about the beginning of April I went into Norfolk to see my daughter, Mrs Dashwood, during her confinement Mrs Dashwood is my daughter, and Lady Astley is the sister of Mr Dashwood When I first heard of any surmise or report to the disadvantage of Lady Astley, it was the Thursday before this event (the elopement) took place It was in the month of July On hearing these reports, I wrote a letter to Mr Elwyn, stating what I had heard about Mr Garth The Rev Mr Elwyn is the confidential friend of Sir Jacob Astley He is chaplain in the family I addressed two letters to him on the subject, one to Melton Constable, and one to London I did not see Sir Jacob until he sent for me at ——— I found him in a dreadful condition From what I have observed since this event, as well as before, I believe that Sir Jacob's affection had not in the least abated

Cross-examined by Mr. Serjeant VAUGHAN

One of my daughters is in the habit of living with Sir Jacob and his lady She resided with them two years Generally some one of the family was there Upon her marrying Mr Sparkes, Miss Blanche (another of my daughters) went to reside with Sir Jacob The age of Lady Astley was twenty-two when she was wed, she might be more She was, I think, about a year and a half older than Sir Jacob, he is now 29 She may be now about 30 or 31 I never saw so happy a couple—I never witnessed those little differences which happen in the best-regulated families He is a good temper—not capable of being betrayed into any thing that he would have reason to regret through his temper I never saw any act of intemperance in Sir Jacob I never knew them to have high words and decidedly never saw blows between him and his lady I have a house in Cavendish-square I resided there when they married, in 1819 I never heard any noise or disturbance in their room, nor did I ever see any thing unpleasant at the dining-table I never perceived her leave the dinner-table suddenly when a gentleman, named Pratt, was there. I remember they were at Holding's Hotel They generally dined with me every day I have no recollection at any time of her leaving my house suddenly to go to the hotel, and Mr Pratt offering to accompany her The occurrence is very unusual I am clear and positive that it never took place in my presence Nothing like high words passed between them, and certainly not personal violence I never was called to her bed-chamber in consequence of a quarrel between her and Sir Jacob He was in the habit of being at Lord Stafford's I never had the honour of dining with Lady Jerningham, but I have met them in parties I have no recollection of

14

being called to the bed-room of Sir Jacob and his lady.
No such occurrence ever took place, I never went to the
bed-room in consequence of something unpleasant having
taken place I never heard Lady Astley complain in my
life of his ill-treatment, his violence or his temper I
never heard any thing occurring unpleasant, except a differ-
ence of opinion about going to town a week sooner, or of
a trifling dispute like that I have never heard her complain
of his attentions to other ladies On no occasion have I had
any reason to believe that there was any interruption to
their happiness I remember their being at Tonbridge with
Mrs Sparkes, perhaps a month, or a fortnight I do not
know that Sir Jacob was there forty-eight hours She had
been unwell, and was recommended, I believe, to go to
Tonbridge I heard nothing about a dispute there Miss
Agnes, now Mrs Sparkes, was at Tonbridge During the
whole time I was at Melton Constable, Sir Jacob was there
I was not in London last year Sir Jacob, I believe, was at
several elections which took him out of town I will undertake to say, that I never remonstrated with him on his attention to other ladies It never was a subject of complaint
from her ladyship

Re-examined by Mr Serjeant T<small>ADDY</small>

I think Lady Astley went to Tonbridge with both her sons
One of the children is four, and the other nearly two years
of age I was abroad at the time, and can't say whether
at that time she was disappointed in the birth of another
child

Mrs Agnes Sparkes examined by Mr D<small>ENMAN</small>

I am sister to Sir Jacob Astley, and was married in Sept
1825 Before that time I had resided two years in the family of Sir Jacob During that time there were several
excursions I was with her whilst she was at Tonbridge
It was for about a month I don't know what was the
reason of her visit, or that she was unwell While I was
with them I should say they were very much attached, and
lived very happily together Sir Jacob was a tender husband, and Lady Astley an affectionate wife and a kind mother to her children I never saw any alteration in that
state I have frequently visited them, and have called
once or twice while in town and I never saw any change
in their conduct towards each other I was not very well
Lady Astley called on me, but not so frequently as I thought
she might have done I left town in June

Cross-examined by Mr Serjeant W<small>ILDE</small>

I first resided with them after their marriage, in 1823, and
went with her to Tonbridge in 1825 I should think Sir
Jacob was there for about a week, but was absent the

greater part of the time I do not know that Lady Astley frequently complained of his absence, and wished his return When we came to town we went to visit Lady Ely Sir Jacob did not accompany us there During the two years I was there, Sir Jacob was not frequently absent, but was always at home with Lady Astley They lived in a state of uninterrupted happiness I was in Hereford-street with her once I do not remember any quarrel, nor do I remember that on one occasion their conduct was such as to cause me to shed tears I do not recollect Sir Jacob on one occasion jumping up from the dinner table, with a knife in his hand I know Mr Bumford but cannot say that I remember that on any occasion I left the room distressed, in consequence of remarks made by Sir Jacob about Mr. Bumford I never remember any personal conflict I never saw him rise with a knife in his hand, or behave in such a manner as to cause me to be disturbed Sir Jacob might have made some remarks about Mr Bumford, but I remember no occasion on which those remarks made Lady Astley uneasy, or caused me to shed tears I decidedly never saw her with her hand cut Sir Jacob had a house in Hereford-street in 1825

Miss Astley examined by Mr SCARLETT

I resided at Sir Jacob's in town, in April last when they came from Melton Constable, and continued to reside with them until this event took place I had been several times to Melton with my brother, and had had an opportunity of observing their conduct, he always treated her with the greatest affection, and appeared to be particularly attached, and it was certainly returned by her He had recently purchased a house in Grosvenor-street, and this was the first time they had come to reside in it Sir Jacob had a large establishment, and every comfort in the world The two children lived with their mother, who appeared to be particularly attached to them I never observed any thing unbecoming an affectionate wife She had great beauty and very agreeable manners, and was a particular favourite in the family The two families the Astleys and the Dashwoods lived in great harmony together Sir Jacob came to town soon after Lady Astley and made arrangements about the furniture I have no recollection of the precise time when he came to town I should think about a fortnight after I continued to live with them when he came to town, and continued with his wife while he was gone to Seaford which I should think was for about three days A house was taken at Worthing for three weeks, for the children They went about the latter end of June I remember when he went to the Bedford and Norfolk elections It was while I was at his house that I first saw Garth He became a frequent visiter in the house He was an officer in the Guards, and was received at Lady Astley's as a visiter, and occasionally dined there He was also in the habit of going with her to the Park I observed that his visits were more frequent during the absence of Sir Jacob Lady Astley sometimes went to Vauxhall, to parties, and to Richmond, with him, he generally formed a part of those parties I saw that he paid her attentions, but they were by no means such as to attract my attention particularly Lady Astley was a great favourite in society Mr Garth continued his attentions while Sir Jacob was at the elections His visits appeared more frequent Lady Astley's brother, the Rev Augustus Dashwood, is in the church, and was in town during a part of the time, and lived principally in Grosvenor-street I remember Mr Elwyn coming to town from Norfolk After he came, the letter arrived which occasioned the agitation Lady Astley went to her room in the course of the day, and remained there I do not recollect the day it was in July An arrangement was made for her to leave town the next day This arrangement appeared agreeable to her I saw Mr Garth on the Sunday previous, in one of the drawing rooms in Grosvenor-street During the time before Mr Elwyn came to town she had been in the habit of going out While Sir Jacob was absent I slept in Lady Astley's apartment On the Monday night I went there between twelve and one o'clock, and did not find her there Mr Elwyn was gone to bed Mr Dashwood lodged at an hotel I made enquiry for her, but she was no where to be found I have not seen her since Mr Garth kept a close carriage it was of chocolate colour He had also an open carriage, and appeared to have an establishment like a man of fortune He has driven myself and Lady Astley in the open carriage It was a phaeton Sir Jacob had been gone to the elections a fortnight previous to the elopement

Cross-examined by Mr BROUGHAM

I should think Mr Garth was about 25 years of age I don't know that the carriage was a hired one He went about a good deal with Lady Astley, frequently to Kensington-gardens, and the Regent's Park and had driven her sometimes to Richmond Sir Jacob was aware of it We went in a large party to Richmond Mr Garth drove Lady Astley by herself He drove her back too We got back between 10 and 11 o clock After that he drove her to Vauxhall I do not know exactly the hour I went to Vauxhall also, and met her walking with him Sir Jacob met us at Vauxhall He was not in town when we went to Richmond in the morning, and had arrived from Norfolk that afternoon I did not go away with Sir Jacob we all came away in a party at the same time Sir Jacob went home in his chariot and was home a very short time before us I do not remember who I went home with it was not with Lady Astley she went home with Mr Garth They went home to Grosvenor-street, and supped Lady Astley and I were present, with Mr Garth and several others Sir Jacop was at supper, and left when the rest of the party broke up I think it was about one o'clock, but I do not exactly recollect the time I remember going to the French play with them Mr Garth Mr Carrol Lady Astley, and myself, formed the party After the play we went to Vauxhall We all went in her ladyship's coach Sir Jacob was not there that night I believe her ladyship and I returned together that night I do not remember whether Sir Jacob was gone to bed I think we set Mr Garth down on the way home He never went with her there, but always met her I remember he once got into her coach in the Regent's-park and drove about with her Sir Jacob was not there I do not recollect that Sir Jacob at breakfast next morning said that he was at Vauxhall, and that they did not see him They were home at any rate by 10 o'clock No conversation of Sir Jacob's having seen her at Vauxhall passed in the morning I think the children were in town while Sir Jacob was at the elections While they were at Worthing Lady Astley proposed going to join them for a fortnight, and she gave no reason for not going She could never have applied to Sir Jacob for money as he had left a large sum with her I do not remember Sir Jacob's saying, " I suppose the Captain is always with you ' I never saw any letter from Sir Jacob to Lady Astley nor have I ever seen any part of one I recollect being at a ball given by a Mrs Hughes Mr Garth was there as was also Lady Astley They were together during the course of the evening Sir Jacob was not at that party I think this was in June

Re-examined by Mr SCARLETT

We expected that Sir Jacob might come home on the night on which he met us at Vauxhall There was a large party of about 19 or 20 persons, ladies and gentlemen A great many returned to Sir Jacob's house, where a regular supper was prepared I was in the carriage with her when Mr Garth got into it in the Regent's Park His horse was restive, and Lady Astley seeing he could not manage it advised him to get off, and get into her carriage, which he did, giving his horse to a servant I think Mr Elwyn did not arrive on that night Lady Astley was in the habit of arriving late on fine summer evenings Mr Garth was more frequently in company with Lady Astley during Sir Jacob's absence, but it was in a guarded way I was not in the phaeton when they went to Vauxhall Mr Garth generally drove her in his phaeton to the Richmond parties I had not the least reason to believe that when Sir Jacob left town he had the slightest suspicion of Mr Garth

Cross-examined by Mr Brougham

My brother was absent the greater part of July He was absent at the Bedford election and other elections

By the Lord Chief Justice

You have been speaking, Madam, of parties to Richmond and Vauxhall, how many of those parties were there, and how many did your brother attend?—We had four parties to Richmond, and Sir Jacob was at only one Captain Garth was at three of these parties at Richmond

By Mr Scarlett, through the Court

Was Sir Jacob in town during any of those three parties, to which you have spoken as being taken in the company of Mr Garth? No, sir, he was not

By the Lord Chief Justice

Did you and Lady Astley return in her carriage, or in that of Mr Garth?—We returned in her ladyship's carriage

Was Sir Jacob informed of his wife being accompanied by Mr Garth when he came to town?—He was

Had you any parties to other places, at which Mr Garth was present during Sir Jacob's absence?—Yes, my Lord, we had two or three parties to Greenwich, at one of which Mr Garth was present

Did your brother express any disapprobation on his coming to town, with Captain Garth's attentions?—I do not think he was aware of them

By the Jury

I saw Lady Astley and Mr Garth at Vauxhall together, but I do not know whether my brother observed them or not I did not meet my brother at all at Vauxhall that evening Mr Gurdon was with Sir Jacob, I believe

The Rev Caleb Elwyn examined by Mr Scarlett

I was a friend of the late Sir Jacob Astley, and lived frequently with the family, which I have known ever since I can remember I remember the present Sir Jacob's marriage with Lady Astley, and have lived invariably at their house in the country and frequently in town, and have had frequent opportunities of seeing the manner in which they lived They appeared to be the happiest couple that could live She appeared to have every reason to be pleased, and conducted herself as a lady of her rank ought to do Sir Jacob appeared to be a very indulgent husband I recollect the circumstance of their going to Leicester in 1826 I accompanied them. Sir Jacob went for the purpose of hunting, Lady Astley was with him Sir Jacob dined from home only twice during the whole time he was there There were about half a dozen single gentlemen residing at an hotel, with whom Sir Jacob was acquainted, and he would sometimes go over to them after he had dined, but invariably returned to drink tea with Lady Astley They left Leicester and went to Melton, from whence they came to town in April The affection appeared rather to increase than diminish When he went hunting, he breakfasted with the gentlemen at the hotel, and Lady Astley breakfasted at home with me, at about ten o clock She had her music and a drawing master she employed her time in walking with me in the public walks until dinner time Sir Jacob took a house in Grosvenor-street, which was not quite finished Lady Astley went to town for the purpose of seeing the furniture I accompanied her Ladyship to town, and returned in a short time afterwards I did not go to town again until the 10th of May Sir Jacob was at home, a good deal employed about the election business I did not go out to parties with them She appeared delighted with her new house and I never saw her happier I returned a few days before Sir Jacob went to Seaford, which was about the 6th of June He was gone only two nights I accompanied him Mr M'Queen was the brother-in-law to Sir Jacob Astley I went as far as Woburn with Sir Jacob when he went to Bedford, and I then went to Cambridge He joined me at his own house at Melton and remained there during the Norfolk election His father and grandfather had represented the county We returned about the 27th of June A house was taken at Worthing for the children I accompanied the children to Worthing, and left them with the servants It was understood that Lady Astley was to join them there Sir Jacob had been in the habit for two years of going to Yarmouth races, and he had agreed to go this year He wished Lady Astley to go with him, but she declined, saying she should prefer being near the children I left on the 8th of July with Sir Jacob and returned on the 19th I arrived in Grosvenor-street at about ten o clock Lady Astley was not at home and the servant said she was gone with Miss Astley into the Park She returned at about half past ten o clock and came into the room with Miss Astley and Mr Garth I had seen him before for a few minutes After some time she said she had received so good an account of the children, that she had not gone to

D

see them Letters had passed between Sir Jacob and Lady Astley Being fatigued, I retired to my room and while getting into bed, I heard the carriage driven up to the door, and heard the servant say it was ready This was about 11 o'clock Lady Astley, Miss Astley, and Mr Garth got into the carriage, and I believe went to Vauxhall, as no other place of amusement could be open at that time On Thursday I had some conversation with Mr Dashwood about going to Worthing I left town on Friday This was after I had received the letter from the Dowager Lady Astley and which caused me to go to Sir Jacob I found a duplicate had fallen into his hands This letter is now destroyed In consequence of that letter it was arranged that I should return to town and that Lady Astley should go into the country, accompanied by her brother Mr Dashwood Before Sir Jacob received that letter I had every reason to believe that he had no suspicion that Mr Garth was carrying on an improper intercourse with his wife He was annoyed by the letter, and could not give credit to it I was not aware that any reports had been spread in Norfolk My object in going to town, was to arrange Sir Jacob's bills, and if Lady Astley had not left town, to escort her to Worthing When I came to town after the reception of the letter, it was to bring the children home from Worthing, and to arrange that Mr Dashwood should take Lady Astley into the country I arrived on Monday, the 24th of July Sir Jacob had written to Mr Dashwood When I came to town, I found she was to leave the next morning I received an excuse from her that she could not see me I went to bed at about twelve o'clock, but was rapped up at about one in order to make a search after Lady Astley, who was missing After searching the house, I went out and inquired where Mr Garth lived, and, on being informed, went to his house He was not at home I have once seen Lady Astley since that was accidentally She has not returned home I left town early on Tuesday morning and went to Sir Jacob I cannot describe the state in which I found him He did not speak but appeared to me in a sort of torpor I never saw any thing in his conduct inconsistent with the tenderest affection for his wife

Cross-examined by Mr Serjeant VAUGHAN —I have been much in Sir Jacob's family I accompanied them to Leicester In an evening he was in the habit of going out for an hour He returned and took coffee with his lady I never heard of any suppings at the Hotel with his hunting acquaintance There was one private race between a horse of his and Sir Edward Mostyn's Lady Astley was present at the race That is the only one which I remember I was in London with them in the spring of last year. In April, May, June, and July, Sir Jacob was absent three days at Seaford and ten days at Norwich election; and from the 8th of July, to the elopement, I was in the habit of dining with Sir Jacob, when in London. I never joined the parties in which he mingled. I never knew that he dined more than once away from home during the time I was in town. Sir Jacob knew Mr Garth, but Lady Astley was not acquainted with him until the 14th of May, 1826. He became acquainted with her, I believe, on calling about a horse.

Thomas Smart examined by Mr Serjeant TADDY.—I am a watchman in St George's parish, Hanover Square. On the night of the 24th of July I went on watch at nine at night, and remained until the following morning. I know both Captain Garth and his carriage. I saw it driving that night in the streets near the square. After one o'clock I saw a carriage stand in Davies-street. I perceived a lady looking out from the balcony of Sir Jacob Astley's house, and she spoke to the coachman. I had not then that night seen Captain Garth. About half-past one I saw a lady get into the carriage. I knew Lady Astley by sight. The lady stepped into the carriage in a hurry, and it drove off. The lady who got in was similar in figure to Lady Astley. The carriage drove off towards Bond-street.

Edward Needham examined by the COMMON SERJEANT.—I am a butler in Sir Jacob's family. On the 24th of July last I was there. On Thursday, the 27th of that month, I went to the Wellesley Inn, at Mary-le-bone green. I saw Captain Garth's servant, and I saw Lady Astley in a room. She was sitting in a chair, and seemed much affected, and very low. I said, "I hope your Ladyship will return." She replied, ' I cannot return.' She repeated this twice. She spoke very low. I said, I hope you will return for the sake of your children.'

Cross-examined by Mr Serjeant WILDE.—I lived about twelve months in the family. I never told my master of Captain Garth's visits. I made no minutes of what took place. Captain Garth was there very often. I never received any instructions from any body respecting their conduct.

Re-examined by the COMMON SERJEANT.—Capt Garth's visits were less frequent when Sir Jacob was at home.

An Ostler at the Wellington Arms stated that Captain Garth and Lady Astley came to that house in July last, but he did not know whether they passed as man and wife.

Sarah Holloway the chambermaid at the Wellington Arms, was then called for the purpose of proving that Lady Astley and Mr Garth lived there as man and wife, when

Mr Serjeant VAUGHAN interposed, saying, that in order

to save time, he would admit that the adultery had taken place

Mary Levett examined by Mr Serjeant TADDY —I am chambermaid at Batt's hotel, Dover-street Two persons came there in the middle of August, whom I now know to be Captain Garth and Lady Astley The Captain had a valet, and her Ladyship a female servant They came on a Saturday, and remained till Thursday

Daniel Elliott, examined by MR. SCARLETT —I am a waiter at St James's Hotel, Jermyn-street Capt Garth and Lady Astley are now living there They came 25th August, and remained seven days then they left and went to Weymouth, and returned to town on the 16th December They now live together as man and wife Captain Garth keeps a carriage and saddle-horses He has a valet, footman, and lady's-maid I do not know the number of stable servants

Cross-examined by Mr Serjeant VAUGHAN —I know not whether the bill be paid or not I do not know whether the carriage is Mr Garth's He has paid two different sums amounting to about 80*l* or 90*l*

Another waiter at the same hotel stated that Mr Garth had now in his pay a coachman, footman, two postillions, and some stable helpers They were all living at the hotel

This was the plaintiff's case

Mr Serjeant VAUGHAN for the defendant, said that if he were possessed of the ordinary feelings of an advocate and a man, he could not approach this case without considerable delicacy Juries were very apt, upon occasions like these, to be up in arms against the adulterer, and their honest indignation was kindled at the very idea of a crime so pernicious in its example, and so destructive to domestic peace He could not, however, help expressing his astonishment that the plaintiff had not satisfied himself with the ordinary means of preferring his suit, but had called in the assistance of two learned gentlemen, who were not usually to be found in that Court, but whose eloquence was thought to be necessary upon this occasion The Jury, however, would judge of the actual merits of the case, by contrasting the evidence on the one side with the evidence upon the other, and the ingenuity and eloquence of his Learned Friend would not at all weigh with them If the only point at issue was, whether the dark deed of adultery had been committed, he should have spared the disgusting details which it was now necessary to lay before the Court, but this was not the only point His client's conduct had been fair, frank, and artless, and it was not attempted to be denied that he had fallen a victim to that fascinating beauty, which no man, whose blood was not snow-broth, could have resisted Thus she had been painted by a great master in matters of this nature—he meant his Learned Friend near him, and the domestic happiness which had thus been destroyed had also been worked up into a highly-wrought picture. Such a picture he had never before witnessed of domestic happiness of which it had been said, that it was " the only bliss of Paradise that had survived the Fall ' It had been represented, that from the moment of the marriage of Sir Jacob and Lady Astley, until the moment of the elopement of the lady, their life had been one continued and unbroken series of all that was happy affectionate and comfortable What a pinnacle of bliss, and what a mighty fall ' and that fall too, be it remembered, altogether unaccounted for Up to this moment the Jury had not heard a syllable in the shape of reason for this adultery The Jury, however he was sure, would not mistake the glowing picture of his Learned Friend for a representation of a matter of fact but would look into the sober realities of life, and consider men as they really existed, and not as eloquence could paint them He trusted he should not be considered as the palliator of adultery much less under the aggravating circumstances with which his Learned Friend had surrounded this case, and if his client had acted in the dark, base, and worthless manner in which he had been represented, he would abandon him at once Upon investigation, however, it would be found that Captain Garth had used none of the arts of the practised seducer even his Learned Friend had himself been compelled to admit that this was not one of those cases in which an old friendship had been violated by the seduction of a wife Within the small space of two months, and this was the utmost length of the acquaintance between Captain Garth and Sir Jacob Astley, the lady of the latter had actually left the arms of this devoted, tender, faithful, and unprecedented husband for those of the Captain He was utterly at a loss to divine from the evidence which had been adduced what single point there was from which the Jury could fairly infer that Captain Garth had seduced the lady of the plaintiff The Jury must know that there was a great deal of tact in the getting up of cases of this description and it had been complained of, in a very high quarter that these cases were never managed properly, or stated fairly Now, had the present case been stated at all fairly ? Who had been called to prove the happy and amiable life which the plaintiff and his wife led ? The mother and the two sisters of the plaintiff, together with the chaplain of the family No other person whatsoever had been called—none of her own family, not even a visiter in the family It generally happened in the ordinary run of families that there was occasionally a something to disturb the tide, however smooth it might generally be—some clouds to obscure now and then the clear sky under which they lived   But here his Learned Friend would have them believe that there never had been even a ripple on the surface, and that from the beginning up to the moment of the elopement there had existed no single fact no one circumstance which would tend to alienate the affections of the wife from her husband.   Was it in the nature of things that the father of a family, an affectionate husband, tender even to a fault, and almost mad in his affection for the partner of his life,—was it in the nature of things that such a man could be deserted by his wife without cause? Women became naturally more and more attached to their husbands as years passed on, especially when there was a family they became endeared to them by long communion, and their children became so many additional bonds of affection and in this case, where all these circumstances existed there was the additional fact, as it had been represented by his Learned Friend of the lady being in herself good and virtuous   There must be something wrong here—something ' rotten in the state of Denmark "—something in the conduct of this devoted husband, which induced the lady to throw herself into the arms of another man, and to leave a husband of considerable wealth for comparative beggary   The fact, as far as it regarded his client was simply this   That he had taken away the plaintiff's wife was most true   The very head and front of his offending had this extent no more   He would not call the attention of the Jury to evidence which had been given on the other side, and which ought to have been given   There was a brother of the lady's, a Mr Dashwood, in town at a very critical time   why was not he called? He would tell them why—because the other side were afraid of some mine exploding   Why were none of the lady's relations called? For the same reason   They had not called a single servant, with the exception of the butler and they did not ask even him upon what terms his master and mistress lived

Mr SCARLETT —Why did not you ask him?

Mr Serjeant VAUGHAN replied, that it was not his business to ask him and he would contend, that coming into Court as the plaintiff did, there ought to have been no disguise on his part but that he ought to have laid his case open to inquiry upon every point   It was, perhaps, a little indiscreet in him (Mr Sergeant Vaughan) to cross-examine Lady Astley about the terms on which the parties lived   It might have prevented them from calling the female servants of the family whose violent interest in matters of this nature, and whose curiosity,—he would not call it a prurient curiosity, —and whose prying disposition made them very valuable witnesses in such cases. He would contend that he was entitled to say from all that had been heard, that the Jury had no right to consider Sir J Astley as the cold sober, sedate and well behaved person which he had been represented to be. He must say, he was bound to say that all his questions to the witnesses had been flatly negatived their representations had been of the most general nature such as that there was nothing on the part of the husband, no bad conduct, to provoke his wife to the step she had taken. Captain Garth was not introduced into Sir Jacob's family until the 14th of last May. He had contracted a slight acquaintance with Sir Jacob in a distant country and called upon him respecting the sale of some horses, upon which occasion he was introduced to Lady Astley. He then became a visiter at the house, and Sir Jacob was represented as being sometimes in the country and sometimes in town. Now, he must observe that most devoted and tender husbands would take care to attend their wives to parties themselves. Where danger lurked, the safest and the seemliest place for a wife was her husband's side. He would ask the Jury if they did not think the frequent absences of this husband highly culpable? An election freak had been talked of and they found that while he was indulging this, he left the field open to any one, and invited what he now sought reparation for which it was quite clear that no husband who had any real affection for his wife would have done. It was incredible that any woman's affections could be undermined in the short space of six weeks except under extraordinary circumstances. Now, as to Vauxhall and such places of amusement, what had been Sir Jacob's conduct? He returns to town upon one occasion, and finds that his lady has gone upon a party of pleasure to Richmond and from thence to Vauxhall. He repairs to the latter place, but how does he meet his wife? Did they find him by his wife's side? No, he went home from Vauxhall in a sulky manner and left his lady to return with Captain Garth. It might be said that he did not see his wife there but having heard that she was in the gardens, what husband would not have searched for her? It was quite clear, however that he had seen her, and even if he had not, was the meeting as it had been described, any thing like that of a tender affectionate and devoted husband? Was not this the conduct of a man who had other objects of pursuit in view, and those too of a very different nature? He would presently show what these objects were. It would be found that the plaintiff had rudely broken every sacred tie of affection between himself and his lady and that his whole conduct was calculated to make her fly to those arms which were not polluted as she knew her husband's had been. He would now openly declare the nature of the defence which he was about to set up

Sir Jacob's conduct had been of a most profligate description He would willingly spare the Jury the details, but it was impossible to do so , all he could do was to make them as little disgusting as possible , and for this purpose he should content himself with samples, rather than produce the whole

WITNESSES FOR THE DEFENCE

[The Learned Serjeant then went on to detail the particulars of the evidence which he was about to adduce, for which we refer our readers to the evidence itself below] He then went on to observe, that if he established these facts, there could be no question about damages If the wife had fallen, whose fault was it ? Had Captain Garth seduced her ? If so, why were there no letters produced, no private meeting pointed out ? The fact was, that Captain Garth had fallen a victim to a lady, whose beauty was as great, and whose manners were as fascinating as they had been described by his Learned Friend And what claim had Sir Jacob now for recompense when his own profligate conduct had extinguished every spark of affection in his wife, and induced her to believe that he had no longer any claims upon her duty ? His Learned Friends had adopted a very strange mode of obtaining damages They had called witnesses to prove that Captain Garth could afford to pay them, and those witnesses were servants, who swore that the Captain had paid two bills at an hotel, one of 30l and the other of 50l and that he was possessed of carriages and horses Now the plain matter of fact was, that Captain Garth was merely a half-pay lieutenant in a dragoon regiment He begged that the Jury would not mistake him If it could be made out that his client had seduced a good and virtuous woman from the path of rectitude, it did not matter how poor he was, and if he could not pay in purse, he must pay in person There was not, however, a tittle of evidence from which the seduction could be inferred He would not detain them any longer, but conclude by asking the Jury whether a husband who had been guilty of such conduct as Sir Jacob Astley's, could expect any thing else from his wife but one of those unhappy instances of dereliction from duty which he was afraid were but too common in the present state of society

Mary Richardson was then called She now lived at Derby , lived at Leicester in part of the year 1826 Knew Sir Jacob Astley Saw him at Leicester in the year 1826 Knew the Bell inn, at Leicester , had seen Sir Jacob Astley there, and also at her own house Knew females of the names of Spawforth, Webster, and Burbidge Had seen them in company with Sir J Astley at her house Had seen Sir Jacob at her house many times Went with Sir Jacob into a private room at the Bell Inn Lady Astley lodged a few doors off Sir J Astley saw these girls at her house in a private room Spawforth and Burbidge support themselves by making caps and bonnets Men and women were in the habit of resorting to her house

Mr Serjeant VAUGHAN —For criminal purposes ?

LORD CHIEF JUSTICE —You have no right to answer that, unless you like

Witness declined answering the question, and continued —These women lived in her house to do her work Sir Jacob Astley and other gentlemen came to her house, " a larking " There were no

other women living in her house   Could not tell how often Sir Jacob
came there "larking"   He always gave money   She received money
from Sir Jacob when she went to him at the Bell Inn   When Sir
Jacob came to her house, he gave her a sovereign to fetch some wine
He went into another room, were there was a bed   Did not know
how long he remained there   The two girls went up with them, and
upon their return she went up to the bed-room, and found the door
locked   She quitted Leicester in March   Sir Jacob was never at her
house after the night of the races   Could not tell the month in which
the races took place   Remembered the day of that race between Sir
Jacob's horse and Sir Edward Mostyn's   Did not recollect if any of
these girls were at the Bell Inn on the night of that day   Was on the
race-course with these two girls, and saw Sir Jacob with Lady Astley
in a carriage   Sir Jacob kissed his hand to them from the carriage,
and said, that he would come and give them a treat that night   Recollected Spawforth and Burbidge coming home that night   They were
quite sober   They never got drunk   She had been twice at the Bell
Inn to Sir Jacob Astley

Cross-examined by Mr SCARLETT —She was now living at Derby
Went from Leicester to her mother's at Norwich   Never told this
story till she was fetched by some gentleman from Derby   Did
not know where she was brought to in London   Was now living
in London   but did not know where   never had told the story
until the present moment in Court   Meant to swear to that   Did
not know the name of the gentleman who fetched her from
Derby   Nor recollected that she was living t the Golden-cross, Char-
ing-cross   No gentleman came and took down her examination since
she came to the Golden-cross   The three women beforementioned accompanied her to town   Did not know what she and they were brought
to town for   Did not know who the other gentlemen were who came
to her house with Sir Jacob Astley   They came about half-past nine,
stayed about two hours   had no idea of their names   Sir Jacob always
gave her a sovereign to fetch wine with , the other gentlemen gave her
money also, about half a sovereign   Did not know Captain Garth,
did not know Mr Howard   Was twice at the Bell Inn with Sir
Jacob Astley, it was between the hours of five and six in the evening   The person who served the paper (the subpœna) on her, only
asked her if she knew Sir Jacob Astley   and if he had ever been at
her house   She had not said in a previous part of her examination
that she never told the story to any one until she came into Court   She
said that she had never told it to any body in London   Nobody had
given her any money to come there , she was taken to the Three Crowns
at Leicester, were she found the two girls   She told the gentleman
who brought her, more than she would have told him if she had known
what he wanted her for   Sir Jacob Astley was in an open carriage on
the race-course   Lady Astley was in the carriage   Besides her, there
were two gentlemen in the carriage   Did not know who they were.
Did not speak to Sir Jacob then   Was too modest to speak to Sir
Jacob before his wife   The other young ladies with her did not say
any thing to Sir Jacob   Did not recollect any particular words that
Sir Jacob used   He said nothing about "gallows"   Would swear
that he said nothing except that he would give them a treat at night.
It was broad daylight and there were many people about

Mary Ann Webster examined by Mr BROUGHAM —Lived at Leicester, knew Mrs Richardson, had been at her house Never saw Sir J Astley there Recollected the private race Was on the course with Mrs Richardson, Miss Spawforth, and Miss Burbidge Saw Sir Jacob in the carriage with his wife and two or three gentlemen Sir J Astley saw them, kissed his hand to them, and said he would treat them in the evening Also saw Sir J Astley on the course on foot The carriage was standing in sight with Lady Astley in it Sir Jacob took the hook of his whip, and hooked up their petticoats He laughed and talked with them He said they were ' gallows ones " He said something else it might begin with a ' B " Saw Sir Jacob again that evening by the Bell Inn gates There was another gentleman with him, and two women came down the street, and followed them into the inn She did not go in herself

Cross-examined by Mr Scarlett —Did not know the name of the other gentleman with Sir Jacob Astley Did not know Captain Garth, nor the names of any of the gentlemen in the carriage Did not go into the Bell Inn, but only stood at the gates talking to Sir Jacob There was nothing particular doing at the Bell that evening She never made any secret of this occurrence Perhaps she had told it as often to females as to gentlemen Had seen a gentleman of the name of Howard He came to her at Leicester And he then asked her if she knew Sir Jacob Astley ? She told him this story Had never seen him since she came to town until that day Told him what Mrs Richardson had told her about Sir J Astley, and he went to Derby to fetch her, in consequence of that information Thought Mr Howard came to town by the same coach with them Told Mr Howard of Mrs Richardson keeping a house which Sir J Astley used to frequent, and he said he would fetch Mrs Richardson Mr Howard was on the coach when it changed horses, and dined in the same room with them Mrs Richardson told Mr Howard in her presence, that she had been in a bed-room twice with Sir Jacob Astley She went with Mr Howard to Derby to fetch Mrs Richardson Mr Howard then asked Mrs Richardson whether she knew Sir Jacob Astley, and she answered " that she ought to know him ' Knew that Mr Howard did not sleep in the same house with Mrs Richardson, and that she slept in a house where Mr Howard would not be allowed to come Mrs Richardson was now a respectable woman Knew that she once kept a house to which people used to resort Was up at work all the night before she started for town Mrs Richardson did not go to bed at all that night either She was on the sofa, because she expected to start early the next morning Would swear that she did not know where Mr Howard spent that evening

By Mr Brougham —Was a dress-maker by business, and in consequence of having lost time by going to Derby with Mr Howard, was obliged to work all night to complete an order before she set off for town Saw the women who went into the Bell Inn with Sir Jacob Astley and the other gentleman come out again They were making a noise near Lady Astley's windows They were drunk

By the Court —The Bell was a fashionable inn Meant to swear positively that Sir Jacob Astley was allowed to take two common women there, and make them drunk There were also two other women I out altogether Remained by the Bell Inn long enough to see them come out again drunk

Charlotte Spawforth knew Mrs Richardson Had been at her house in the company with ladies and gentlemen Knew Sir Jacob Astley Had seen him at Leicester Had seen him at Mrs Richardson's Was never in private with him there There were other gentlemen with him at Mrs Richardson's Sir Jacob Astley drank wine there with the ladies and gentlemen Sir Jacob Astley, after drinking wine, went into a private room with Miss Burbidge It was a bedroom Was at the race-course with Mrs Richardson and Miss Burbidge Saw Sir J Astley there He was in a carriage with Lady Astley and two gentlemen He kissed his hand to them, and promised to give them a treat that night They were at a short distance from the carriage Before he got into the carriage he came up to them on foot He had a whip in his hand, and with the hook of it, he caught hold of the bottom of Miss Burbidge's frock Had heard Sir Jacob Astley talk to other ladies Did not know whether those ladies were loose girls Paid no attention to what he said Never was at the Bell

By Mr Serjeant Taddy —Walked back with Miss Burbidge to the Bell Sir Jacob Astley said several times from the carriage that he was going to treat them Did not sit up all night at Leicester Could not tell the name of the place she came from that morning

Here the proceedings of the Court were interrupted by a disturbance in the crowd

The Lord Chief Justice ordered the tipstaff to take the offending parties into custody, and desired any person who had witnessed their conduct to come forward

A barrister whose name we could not learn, said that he had seen them conducting themselves very improperly

The Lord Chief Justice ordered the barrister to be sworn

The barrister then pointing to one of two persons in custody, said that he had called a gentleman a d—d rascal

The accused described himself as Captain Hatton, of the Royal Navy He said that he was really so very much pressed that he could not help letting out the expression, for which he was very sorry

Mr Chitty said that the other one refused to let him pass to his seat

The second person described himself as Captain Collier of the Royal Navy, and also advanced the excessive crowd and pressure as his apology

The Lord Chief Justice said, that as they had apologized he could not press the matter any farther

The examination of Charlotte Spawforth was then resumed The other girls, Mrs Richardson, and herself were all living together now. Could not tell where Had never been in London before

By the Court —Was sure she saw Sir Jacob Astley pull the girl's petticoats with his whip Did not hear him say any thing about " gallows ones" Was close by, about two or three yards from Burbidge at the time

Lucy Burbidge examined by Mr Serjeant Vaughan —Lived at Leicester Had lived there 11 years Knew Sir J Astley Became acquainted with him last March Saw him first at Mrs Richardson's He came with another gentleman He was down stairs There were other girls in the room besides He remained in the room about half an hour He then went up stairs with her into a bed-room Remained there with him for about half an hour Was acquainted with him then Knew him then He took liberties with her Did not think that she had a right to answer whether he knew her as man and wife He did not give her any thing Never was with him but that once He said he should see her again that Friday week, and he was then to have made her a present, but he went away *from Leicester* without performing his promise Saw Sir J Astley in an open carriage, on the race-course with Lady Astley He got out of the carriage, and said, "Girls, I shall be with you to-night, and give you a treat" He said nothing else He went to the carriage again, and put his hand to his mouth, and " blowed " a kiss to them

Cross-examined by Mr DENMAN —Lady Astley could not see him blow this kiss They were three or four yards behind the carriage at this time Could not say which of the young lady's petticoats he pulled up with his whip, but was quite sure it was not her's Had not seen Sir J Astley more than once at Mrs Richardson's He gave them a treat one night afterwards The gentlemen in the house called him Sir Jacob Astley Besides this, she had seen him at the races, and knew him again

Sir Edward Mostyn examined by Mr Serjeant WILDE —Was at Leicester in the early part of the year 1826 Sir Jacob Astley was there at that time Perfectly recollected the race Had to the best of his belief often seen Sir Jacob at Mrs Richardson's, but could only speak distinctly to one occasion Was staying at the Bell Inn Sir Jacob Astley often came to the Bell after dinner On one occasion several women came up to him and Sir Jacob Astley, as they were standing at the door of the Inn Walked in, and Sir Jacob Astley also came in shortly afterwards The women followed him into the room The women had something to drink, and they had a good deal of trouble to get them out of the room When they had been put out, they forced themselves in again a second time The nearest way to where Lady Astley lodged would be through the back of the Bell Inn The distance that way was about 500 or 600 yards, but by the road it was considerably farther The women were extremely riotous Recollected one occasion upon which he was with Sir Jacob Astley on the race course, and Sir Jacob spoke to two or three women Sir Jacob Astley had a whip in his hand, and endeavoured to hook up the petticoats of one of the girls Made some observation to Sir Jacob Astley about it To the best of his recollection it was one of caution, lest Lady Astley might see him It was certainly something to that effect

Cross-examined by Mr SCARLETT —It was the wine that was left after dinner, which the girls had Did not recollect that Sir J Astley dined at the Bell more than once Did not recollect whether Sir J Astley had dined there that day There were seven or eight girls with them at Mrs Richardson's They might have remained there an hour or two Could not recollect whether they all came away together Was quite sober at the time As far as thinking went, did *not think that Sir J Astley had any connexion with any woman there* Gentlemen who dined at the Bell often went to Mrs Richardson's They certainly went there frequently, but could not say whether often enough to constitute a habit There were several girls in the house There was either wine or spirits There might have been both

Could not recollect the day of the month on which the race took place
Knew Captain Garth Knew him first at Leicester, at the Bell, when
the hounds were in the neighbourhood Could not say whether
Captain Garth was at the race Conceived Captain Garth to be perfectly well known in Leicester On the day of the race there was a
dinner at the Bell Each person paid for his own dinner There was
music at the Bell one evening Could not swear, but thought that it
was on the evening of the race Lady Astley was at the Bell on the
night of the music, in Sir Jacob Astley's company Several of them
drank tea with Lady Astley, in an adjoining room

By a Juryman—I thought that Sir Jacob Astley paid for the liquor
at Mrs Richardson's

By the Court—Recollected that Sir Jacob Astley was out of his
sight, and in another room, with one of the girls while he was there
Had said, that as far as thinking went, he did not think that Sir J
Astley had had connexion with any woman at Mrs Richardson's, because he had no positive proof of it

The LORD CHIEF JUSTICE here called for Burbidge, and asked the
witness if she were the girl with whom Sir J Astley had retired?

Sir Edward Mostyn—That was certainly one of the girls that
were present, but I can't swear that it was she with whom Sir Jacob
retired

Captain Bulkeley, examined by Mr BROUGHAM—Was a captain in
the Guards Knew Sir Jacob Astley Had been at Mrs Richardson's According to the best of his recollection, he had not been there
more than once Saw Sir Jacob Astley there There were several
women and some liquor there Sir Jacob Astley left the room with
one of the girls, and might have been absent, perhaps a quarter of
an hour

Cross-examined by Mr SCARLETT—There were four or five of
them at Mrs Richards ns Knew Captain Garth, never told him of
this circumstance Did not recollect whether Sir Jacob Astley dined
at the Bell that day There was a row in the street, and they all
went out to see what was the matter, it was near Mrs Richardson's
house, and so they went in Did not recollect that any one in particular proposed to go into the house The door of the house opened
into the sitting-room Did not retire with any lady himself Went
into the house because the others did Stayed there about a quarter
of an hour or 20 minutes I thought he came away by himself It
was purely by accident that he went to the house Did not know the
girl with whom Sir Jacob retired Saw Sir Jacob come down again.
There might have been some laughing and joking about it, but did
not recollect that there was Saw no other person besides Sir Jacob
Astley retire with a girl

Captain Rich, examined by Mr CHITTY—Knew Sir Jacob Astley,
Leicester, and Mrs Richardson's Saw Sir Jacob there once Possibly more than once, but could not swear to how often certainly
once Believed it was on the day of the race Was pretty confident
that Sir Edward Mostyn was there Sir Jacob Astley remained there,
perhaps half an hour There was wine or spirits, and several women
there Sir Jacob Astley retired with one of the girls, and was absent
with her probably a quarter of an hour Sir Jacob Astley went up
stairs with the girl The staircase opened immediately out of the

room where they were sitting Did not exactly remember seeing them come down again

By the Court —Sir Jacob Astley was perfectly sober at the time

Elizabeth Raven examined by Mr Serjeant Vaughan —Lived at Yarmouth, knew Sir Jacob Astley Was at the Yarmouth races, saw Sir Jacob Astley there on the first day of the races, had had no previous acquaintance with him Sir Jacob Astley asked her for her card and she refused to give it him He then asked her where she lived, but she did not tell him She never saw him in her own house, or in the house of any other person Never saw him at any other time but on the course Never saw him at the Vauxhall-gardens Would swear distinctly that she did not see him after the first day of the races Did not see him talking to any other women Should scarcely know him again if she were to see him All she knew about him was that he was a *small gentleman*

Mr Serjeant Vaughan —Ah, and so is Captain Garth

Susan Paul, examined by Mr Serjeant Wilde —Lived at Yarmouth Saw Sir Jacob Astley there last year, in July, both at the Jetty and at Vauxhall-gardens Was addressed by him, and he gave her money to go to the theatre with He took no liberties with her person Did not see him more than twice He did not kiss her on either occasion He made no appointment with her Saw him the second time in the Vauxhall-gardens It was a public place in which Sir Jacob Astley gave her the money It was in Chapel-street He did not talk to her for more than five minutes

By Mr Scarlett —The Vauxhall-gardens are places of great resort Sir Jacob Astley gave her 5s She did not ask him for it There were other gentlemen in his company at the time Had never seen him till then Had never seen him since that day Had never mentioned this to any one until she was asked to come to London by Mr Coble, of Yarmouth The gentlemen on the race-course told her it was Sir Jacob Astley or else she should not have known who he was

Mr Thomas Baker examined by Mr Brougham —Knew Sir Jacob Astley by sight Was at Yarmouth at the last races saw Sir Jacob there Saw him in the gardens Saw him talking to women as he passed them Could not say whether they were loose women They certainly had not the appearance of ladies He talked to them in a familiar way They appeared to him to be the contrary to modest women

Rose Constable —I live in St Stephens's, Norwich I can't say that I know Sir Jacob Astley, but once a party of gentlemen who had been hunting came to my house, and I was afterwards told that one of them was Sir Jacob Astley I never saw the gentlemen before or since

Mr Scarlett objected to any evidence of this nature, where it was clear the witness could not identify any of the persons that came to her house

Mr Serjeant Vaughan —Let her stand down for the present We shall come to the identity by and by

The Hon Henry Jerningham, examined by Mr Serjeant Vaughan —Did not know Mrs Rose Constable Knew that there was such a house as her's at Norwich Never saw Sir Jacob Astley at that house

Mr George Jerningham, examined by Mr Serjeant Vaughan —
Knew where Mrs Constable's house in Norwich was. Never saw
Sir J Astley there. Remembered a hunting dinner at Norwich, and
it brought back nothing connected with her house to his mind. He
dined with Sir Jacob at that hunting dinner. The party broke up at
eight o'clock, and went to the play. He came away from the play
with Sir Jacob, and supped with him at the Norfolk hotel. They
separated at about twelve o'clock. Did not sleep at Norwich, but
rode into the country that night. There were several gentlemen at
the dinner, but no ladies.

By Mr SCARLETT —It was a dinner given by Sir J Astley to a
few friends. Did not recollect Sir J Astley and his lady visiting his
father.

The Hon Henry Jerningham was recalled —He visited Sir Jacob
and Lady Astley, at Melton, about three years ago.

By the COURT —They seemed to live like other people, and to be
on very good terms with each other.

Mr Elwyn recalled, and examined by Mr SCARLETT —He perfectly remembered the day of the race between Sir E Mostyn and Sir
J Astley. On the night of that day there was music at the Bell, and
Sir J Astley fetched Lady Astley to hear the band. He went also.
They remained there about three hours, and all three of them went
home together. Was confident this was the day of the race. Was
in the carriage the whole of the time on the race-course. Would swear
positively that he did not hear Sir Jacob Astley address any women
there. He heard nothing about his promising to treat any women.

By Mr Serjeant VAUGHAN —He could not have seen Sir J Astley
blow a kiss, if he had done so, but he must have heard any thing
that Sir J Astley said.

By a JUROR —The head of the carriage was not up.

The defence was here closed.

Mr SCARLETT said that the time had now arrived at which he was
to address the Jury in reply. He would never defend conduct in any
client at which his own conscience revolted, and he would not stand
up as the palliator of any crimes which his own heart taught him to
despise. He would not have attempted to defend Sir Jacob Astley, if
it had been proved that he was the profligate character which his
Learned Friend had proposed to demonstrate him to be, and he must
call upon the Jury to distinguish between an habitual and flagrant
course of adultery and licentiousness, and the fact that upon one
solitary occasion Sir Jacob Astley might possibly have been betrayed
into an act of indiscretion. He called upon the Jury to recollect with
whom Lady Astley was now living. Was it not likely that she would
be willing to give her paramour all the information in her power, in
order to enable him to make a case? She could name the witnesses,
the times, the places of offence and crime, if there had been any, and
yet with all these advantages what sort of evidence had Captain
Garth brought? He (Mr Scarlett) had brought testimony to prove
the kindness and tenderness of the plaintiff as a husband, and his
learned friend had not disproved that testimony. His Learned Friend
had asked why the family of the lady had not been produced. Had
not the event proved that if he had done so, he should have taken up
the time of the Court uselessly? Had his Learned Friend shaken in
the slightest degree that testimony which had been brought? He

had not, and yet he wished for more. Besides this, he would not wantonly wound the feelings of any part of that lady's family, who must already be overwhelmed with distress at her conduct. He would not call her mother and her sisters; there was no occasion for them. But how had Capt. Garth acted? Had he shown any delicacy? No, he had dived into brothels, to rake up mere suspicion. Sir Jacob Astley had declared to his counsel, and to all around him, that he was innocent, and so convinced was he that the allegations of immorality could not be supported against him, that he had resolved to stand the test, and dare his adversaries to the proof. The Learned Counsel then proceeded to comment upon the evidence, and having gone through the whole of it, said that he would now call the attention of the Jury more minutely to the conduct of Captain Garth. It was clear what his intentions were. He had no doubt promised the victim whom he had seduced, the reparation of marriage, in the event of a divorce, and now in his defence in this Court he adopted a line of conduct which he hoped would prevent him from being able ever to make that promised reparation. He had at once attempted to defend himself, and so to vilify the plaintiff's character, as to prevent his obtaining a divorce, and his pledges to Lady Astley would thus still exist, and not be forfeited. Thus it was that he seduced deceived, and then betrayed his victim. He never would believe that Captain Garth, a person moving in the first circles, and esteemed, as it was said, by many and powerful friends, could have brought himself to adopt such a defence for the mere purpose of saving a few hundreds. Would a man of honour condescend to set up such a defence as this, if he had not some secret motive in view? And what motive was more probable than this? He would not call Captain Garth's inclination for Lady Astley by the name of love, that passion was of a brighter and purer kind, but this was mere animal lust, and to defend it, he seemed to have said "If I cannot gain my point by fair I will by foul means. I will not leave a stone unturned—a stratagem untried. I will move Heaven and earth, and descend to any even to the lowest and basest means.

> " Flectere si nequeo superos,
> ——— Acheronta movebo."

Was not this adding another injury to the great one which he had already committed? He trusted that the Jury would show by their verdict that such a dishonourable and disgraceful defence as this was, would increase rather than lessen the damages, and that the wretch who robbed another of his wife, and then attempted to deprive the man whom he had thus deeply injured, of character too, would not be able to shield himself from the visitation which he so richly merited. He trusted that the Jury would moreover prove by the verdict which they were about to give, that it did not follow that because an adulterer had watched the husband into a brothel upon one solitary occasion, he was for that reason justified in satisfying his lust upon the person of the wife.

THE JUDGE'S CHARGE TO THE JURY

The Lord Chief Justice BEST *then proceeded to address the Jury to the following effect.* —This is a case, Gentlemen of the Jury, of the utmost importance to the parties concerned. It is fit that I should remove out of the way topics with which you have nothing to do in the consideration of your verdict It has been said, that if you give a verdict with small damages, it will prevent the plaintiff from prosecuting a suit with success elsewhere With that you and I have nothing whatever to do What may become of this case in another place has nothing to do with your verdict You are called upon for a decision according to the evidence, utterly regardless of the consequences that may result to the plaintiff The same Learned Counsel who addressed that observation to you, to which I have adverted, likewise observed, that this defence was not set up for the purpose of lightening the damages which otherwise you might have been disposed to give, but that it was brought forward in order to exonerate the defendant from the promises which he had made to the lady whom he had seduced If such, indeed, be his object, a baser wretch does not exist on the face of the earth than this defendant If the defence be intended to protect him from engagements which he thinks he should be compelled to perform, in every point of view—if such were really his desire, the defence would be most scandalous, most disgraceful, most abominable The two points to which it will be first necessary to direct your attention, and which must be satisfactorily proved to your minds, are—first, that Lady Astley was married to Sir Jacob; and secondly, that adultery has been committed The latter fact has been admitted, and the former has been clearly established Your verdict must therefore pass for the plaintiff, and the only remaining question is, as to the amount of damages which you will give That is a question entirely for your decision—with it I have nothing to do My duty is to state such observations as my experience enables me to state, arising from the evidence But after having stated the remarks which I think it proper to offer, the decision of the amount of damages is left entirely in your own hands I am anxious that you may have no consideration in your minds foreign to this question You are on your oaths to say, from the statement of facts, upon the evidence given, what the amount of the damages shall be On the part of the plaintiff, sufficient proof has been offered, as I before observed, to entitle him to your verdict With respect to the evidence on his behalf, his most respectable parent, the Dowager Lady Astley, has shown to you his station of life He is a man of high rank, a Baronet, and of an ancient family The lady whom he married is the daughter of a Baronet, and has a brother married to his sister She was a little older than he at the time of their union, a year or two, but her great beauty, it appears, overbalanced that objection Their acquaintance commenced in early life, when he was at Oxford, and the marriage was solemnised with the perfect consent of both these most respectable families Such was the esteem in which she was held, that it was the cause, as you have heard, of another connection in the family The Learned Judge next observed upon the evidence of Lady Astley, Mrs Sparkes, her daughter, and the Rev Mr Elwyn, as to the affection which they stated to have subsisted between Sir Jacob and his Lady previous to the elopement, and thus continued —All these witnesses concurred in proving that it was impossible for any couple to live more happily than Sir Jacob and Lady Astley did, until that unfortunate connection was formed with the defendant These witnesses were all asked respecting the irritability of temper which Sir Jacob was said to have betrayed towards his wife on various occasions, and not one fact of that description was proved to exist. It was likewise

r

asked if he had not taken up a knife and ran towards his wife, in a passion, and if he had not used language of a violent nature towards her These questions have received invariable answers in the negative from each of the witnesses to whom they were put, with a degree of indignation, if 1 may so express myself, that such an imputation should for a moment have had existence Before I pass on to other parts of the case, I cannot forbear mentioning this observation —If there were any foundation for those charges, they were capable of being proved Witnesses might have been called to prove these facts Gentlemen, it has been frequently observed by Judges, that there is as much to be collected sometimes from the absence of witnesses, who might have deposed to certain facts, as if they were present It may not be improper to ask, where were those facts, if true, obtained, to which those ladies were subjected to examination ? They came from the wife of the plaintiff, unless they be a mere imagination of the persons whose duty it is to get up this defence In either case it was an endeavour to heap up injuries on a man who had already been deeply injured I hope adulterers will learn that when they have gratified their passions, they cannot, without calling forth indignation, avail themselves of information obtained through the means which honourable minds would disdain to use When I was at the bar, Gentlemen, I always in painful cases, in which the feelings of families were concerned, avoided, if possible, calling members of those families, if they could be dispensed with With regard to what the highly respectable lady, the mother of the plaintiff, has said, as to her sour temper, it may be open to this remark In the presence of a mother, perhaps parties would not act exactly as they otherwise would in the presence of individuals who had not so intimate a connection—not so great an influence in the family , and therefore it is that I regret that some persons, who were not so nearly united with the plaintiff's family, were not called But above all whom I should like to have seen as a witness is the Rev Mr Dashwood, who was in London at the time that important letter was sent by the Dowager Lady Astley to the Rev Gentleman, whose evidence you have this day heard The evidence of the Honourable Mr Jerningham is important, although he does not describe in so glowing colours as the other most respectable witnesses for the plaintiff do, the manner in which Sir Jacob and Lady Astley lived That Honourable Gentleman said, to use his own words, " that he thought the plaintiff and his wife lived as most people do " From which I collect that he perceived nothing particular in their conduct one way or the other, because I cannot conceive that the witness intended to jest This is the plaintiff's case My Brother Vaughan stated that Sir Jacob Astley was a man of the most profligate habits, and therefore that he was not deserving nor entitled to damages Let it not go forth to the world that profligacy on the part of a husband give countenance to a wife s retaliation It is the duty of a wife " to overcome evil with good "—and to endeavour by all possible means in her power, to correct the bad habits which her husband may have contracted The infidelity of a wife produces consequences far more fatal to her family, to the children which she has borne, than any crime of that sort which the husband may commit But although I state this, for fear it should go forth to the public that if the husband has committed adultery he is not, on that account, entitled to damages if his wife be seduced from him—I add, that where the husband commits adultery, and conducts himself in a scandalous, open, and debauched manner, then, in such a case, he has no right to ask for damages in a Court of Justice The affection which the husband ought to possess for a wife is of a very peculiar description—of such a nature that even the thought of an illicit intercourse gives indescribable pain Do you believe, gentlemen, after what you have heard of this plaintiff's conduct, that his affection for his wife was of so tender and delicate a nature? He has thrown away the jewel which he possessed If those witnesses, the women called for the defendant, are to be believed, he is an habitual adulterer But their stories were full of contradictions Each of them contradicted the other in many circumstances in which they could not come with accounts made up When truth is blended with falsehood, that you cannot say where the one begins and the other ends, how are we to decide? One of these witnesses would have you believe (Mrs Richardson) that two women went into an inn in Leicester, with whom she would insist he committed adultery If the plaintiff had taken a woman there for that, I had almost said beastly purpose, possessing so beautiful and accomplished a wife, he would have been what scarcely a man, however depraved, can be found to be If those witnesses were further to be credited, he had persuaded two abandoned women into the inn, to make them drunk It seems that these women forced themselves into the room, but probably he had before given them some encouragement which, as a married man, it was exceedingly improper to do This also happened within three hundred yards of the place in which his own wife was Supposing that his intention was not to commit adultery, what an act of indiscretion it was! This was not done in a state of intoxication, which, by the bye, is no excuse for crime According to the testimony, which there was not a breath to taint, did he this married man, in the month of March last enter a brothel? He, the only married man of the party, went into the bed-room with a girl, who, to-day, on being confronted, with Sir Edward Mostyn, was acknowledged by him to be of the party, but he could not undertake to say that she was the young woman with whom the plaintiff retired He remained, according to one gentleman's testimony, a quarter of an hour, to another's half an hour, with her It is proper to add, gentlemen, that Sir Edward Mostyn believes that no criminal connection occurred But I beg to ask, for what purpose did the plaintiff retire? It could be for no good one In either case it was shameful Yet it is urged, that it is but in a single instance that the plaintiff had thus acted He, the only married man of the party, retired with a prostitute into a bed-room! The case, however, does not rest here, gentlemen, for we have the testimony of Sir Edward Mostyn that the plaintiff was guilty of the most improper conduct upon the race-course. Such proceedings, on the plaintiff's part, would seem to deserve a madhouse If he kissed his hand to these infamous prostitutes—how disgraceful---how profligate! It is conceded by the Rev Mr Elwyn, that the plaintiff might have done so, without his observing it That gentleman negatives the fact of the plaintiff's having spoken to those women on the race-course It had been positively sworn that he got out of the carriage—in which he left his beautiful wife (for losing whom, it seems, he travelled forty miles, paralyzed, without speaking a word)—conversed with some prostitutes, and using his whip-hook to the petticoats of one of them If the case rested here, is it one calling for damages? Where was the plaintiff in July last? At the races at Yarmouth How did he there act? Inquired of a woman, a stranger to him, for her card, which inquiry she spurned with contempt, and refused him her address There was no reason to disbelieve her testimony It was no fault of his that he was not acquainted with her, and, from high authority, as it must be inferred, he had, "already committed adultery in his heart" He meets another woman in Yarmouth, and how does he treat her? Is it not extraordinary that a married man, a Baronet of great fortune, in the very county in which his property is situated, should accost a girl of that description in the street, to whom he was a perfect stranger? Was this the conduct of a discreet married man —especially of one of high rank—in the place too, where his face was as well known as those noblemen are known in this metropolis who are now sitting on this Bench? One thing I had almost forgot to mention relative to the plaintiff's conduct towards his wife It was for the Jury to say whether Sir Jacob Astley was right in permitting his wife to go about to parties, to Vauxhall, and other places, with a gentleman to whom she had been only introduced a very short time? With long acquaintance I am not inclined to believe it would have been wrong to permit such proceedings, but the acquaintance between these parties was exceedingly limited It had been said that on the very night that the plaintiff came to town he discovered that his wife had gone to Vauxhall with Mr Garth, whom he permitted to drive her home, whilst he went to his residence sulkily in his coach, accompanied by Mr Gordon. You are in possession of the whole case, if you believe the defendant's case, you will give merely nominal damages His misconduct at Leicester and at Yarmouth had been proved by witnesses in the former place of his own rank, and at the latter by those whose testimony was not in the least to be doubted The case, Gentlemen, is in your hands, and you will give such a verdict as you think it merits.

The Jury retired for nearly two hours, and about nine o'clock returned with a verdict for the plaintiff.—

DAMAGES, ONE SHILLING

[Thus Sir Jacob Astley obtained only *Twelve Pence* instead of *Twelve Thousand Pounds,* being the amount at which he had laid the Damages in the declaration]

The Foreman said, that he was desired by the rest of the Jury to declare they deeply regretted that they could not conscientiously mark their detestation of the defendant's conduct by giving heavy damages, but they could not do so, as they considered the plaintiff was not entitled to them, as he had not himself come into court with clean hands.

The Court was crowded to excess at an early hour Several Noblemen and Gentlemen of rank were present, amongst the former were Lords Stafford, Sefton, and Mountford, who sat on the Bench

THE END

Fairburn, Printer,
Broadway, Ludgate-hill